BLIND FAITH
LIVING A LIE

by
Thomas Wilks
Michelle Hicks

LifeWay Press
Nashville, Tennessee

© Copyright 1995 · Convention Press
All rights reserved
ISBN 0-7673-2101-4

Dewey Decimal Classification Number: 291.2
Subject Heading: DOCTRINAL THEOLOGY/CULTS

Unless indicated otherwise, all Scripture quotations in this publication are from the Holy Bible, *New International Version*, copyright © 1973, 1978, 1984 by International Bible Society. Used by permission.

Printed in the United States of America.
To order additional copies of this resource: WRITE LifeWay Church Resources Customer Service, 127 Ninth Avenue, North, Nashville, TN 37234-0113; FAX order to (615) 251-5933; Phone 1-800-458-2772; EMAIL to CustomerService@lifeway.com; ONLINE at www.lifeway.com; or visit the LifeWay Christian Store serving you.

Youth Section
Discipleship and Family Group
LifeWay Christian Resources
of the Southern Baptist Convention
127 Ninth Avenue, North
Nashville, Tennessee 37234-0152

CONTENTS

THE WRITERS
4

INTRODUCTION
5

Chapter 1 Mormons:
    Are They Christians? 8

Chapter 2 Jehovah's Witnesses:
    Are They Knocking On Your
    Door? 26

Chapter 3 Muslims:
    Why Are They So Mysterious?. . 44

Chapter 4 Buddhists:
    A Religion With No God 60

GROUP LEARNING ACTIVITIES
79

THE WRITERS

Thomas Wilks is associate professor of applied ministry and in-service guidance director at Oklahoma Baptist University, Shawnee, Oklahoma. Tom has earned degrees from Louisiana College, New Orleans Baptist Theological Seminary, and Southern Baptist Theological Seminary. Tom has served in many different church leadership positions. He and his wife, Jackie, and their two sons, Bryan and David, attend Immanuel Baptist Church in Shawnee, Oklahoma.

Michelle Hicks is a free-lance youth writer and conference leader. Michelle has earned degrees from the University of North Texas and Southwestern Baptist Theological Seminary. Michelle and Joe have three daughters, Karis, Kali, and Kaia. They attend ClearView Baptist Church in Franklin, Tennessee.

INTRODUCTION

Now faith is being sure of what we hope for and certain of what we do not see (*Heb. 11:1*).

HAVE YOU EVER WONDERED WHY you are a Christian rather than some other religion? What makes a Christian different from a Mormon, Jehovah's Witness, Muslim, or Buddhist? Are we all blindly following the religion we were born into or grew up with?

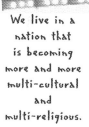

We live in a nation that is becoming more and more multi-cultural and multi-religious.

We live in a nation that is becoming more and more multi-cultural and multi-religious. So, it is even more important that you know what you believe and why. The growing Christian is one who not only has a system of belief, but also has knowledge about those beliefs. It is equally important to know why one rejects other religious beliefs. Many people reject other religions simply because they know nothing about them. It is better to reject a belief on the basis of knowledge.

That is what BLIND FAITH is all about. As a Christian, you need to understand and know what other religions believe. Also, you need to understand why, as a Christian, you cannot accept the *beliefs* of other religions. However, not accepting the beliefs of other religions does not mean you should ignore the *people* who are dedicated to these different beliefs.

You need to know what they believe. This will enable you to better understand them and build relationships with them. As you become more sure of your Christianity, you can discover new ways to share Jesus Christ with people of these religions. Whether that person is Mormon, Jehovah's Witness, Muslim, Buddhist, or other religious belief, you can be the one to explain how

Christianity is different. You can be the one to share the hope that only Jesus Christ can bring to them.

Hopefully, by looking at the beliefs of other religions, you will grow stronger and be more convinced of your own faith in Jesus Christ. Also, you will realize that you do not have a "BLIND FAITH," but are certain of the things you do not see.

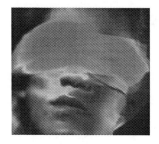

CHAPTER 1
MORMONS: ARE THEY CHRISTIANS?

"Shh! She'll hear you!" whispered Heather.
"So what if she does? I don't care!" Kristi replied.
"Hey, what are you two talking about?" Todd asked.
"We're talking about Melody, that girl over there," Heather whispered as she briefly nodded in Melody's direction. "Did you know she's a Mormon?"
"Yeah? So what is she doing at a Christian church camp?" snarled Kristi.
"That's just it. She thinks she IS a Christian!" snapped Heather.
As they sat watching Melody eat lunch, Todd wondered whether he should get involved in this conversation. After a few seconds, though, he knew he had to say something.
"Somebody needs to talk to Melody about her beliefs. Somebody needs to explain to her that she's not a Christian."
"Well, I don't know enough about Mormonism to talk to her," Kristi paused, "except that they be-

> "That's just it. She thinks she IS a Christian!" snapped Heather.

It can be very difficult to compare what we believe with other religions when we don't know or understand what other religions believe.

lieve that when women die they are eternally pregnant!"
"No way! You're kidding, right?"
"Would I joke about that?"
"That is too weird! Who told you Mormons believe that?"
"I read it in a book. They believe in general salvation, individual salvation, and three different levels in heaven. The highest level makes them gods and eternally pregnant," replied Kristi.
Heather stared at Melody out of the corner of her eye, hoping she wouldn't look her way.
"It sounds like you know a lot more about Mormonism than Heather or I do. So, are you going to talk to her?" Todd asked as he finished eating the last bite of his hamburger.
"Me? Why me?"
"Because you seem to know some of the things that Melody believes as a Mormon. Believe me, you'll be able to understand her a lot better than we will."
"Forget it! She'll try to make it seem like I'm crazy for believing what I believe!"

Have you ever found yourself in a situation like this? You know you need to talk to someone about their beliefs, but are afraid you won't be able to defend your own faith?

It can be very difficult to compare what we believe with other religions when we don't know or understand what other religions believe. It can be especially hard when the person of another religion believes that he or she is a Christian. Like Melody, most Mormons believe they are Christians. How do we know they are not? Look at several basic Mormon beliefs and then determine for yourself.

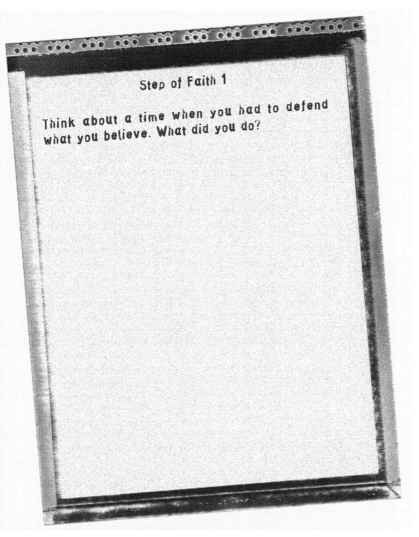

WHAT MORMONS BELIEVE ABOUT THE BIBLE

Mormonism is a religion founded upon the teachings of Joseph Smith (1805-1844). On September 21, 1823, Joseph said he was praying when he saw an angel, Moroni. The angel told him about a set of golden plates that contained the "gospel," which is now Mormon theology. Smith claimed he found the plates buried in a stone box near his home in New York. Mormons believe these golden plates were translated by Smith and are known today as *The Book of Mormon.*

Mormons regard *The Book of Mormon, The Pearl of Great Price,* and *The Doctrine and Covenants* as the Word of God. *The Book of Mormon* is supposedly the history of ancient Americans of Jewish descent who sailed to America about 600 B.C. The people established a civilization in the Western world. The book teaches that Jewish traditions were continued, temples were built to God, spiritual revivals were held, and the Christian church was established.

The Book of Mormon can really confuse a Christian because parts of it sound so much like the Bible.

Mormon doctrine teaches that Joseph Smith translated *The Book of Mormon* accurately. However, the book has been changed nearly 4,000 times. Also, over 27,000 words are from the King James Version of the Bible with approximately 400 verses or portions of verses quoted from the New Testament. *The Book of Mormon* can really confuse a Christian because parts of it sound so much like the Bible. The best thing a Christian can do when looking at *The Book of Mormon* is to have the Bible open for comparison.

Mormons believe that our Bible is in error and unreliable. According to Mormon teaching, the Bible can only be properly interpreted by Mormons and in light of Mormon theology.

As Christians, we believe our Bible is reliable and complete as it is. Nothing has been added or changed. Actually, it is *The Book of Mormon* that is unreliable and incomplete. Even today *The Book of Mormon* is still being changed!

Before going any further in learning about Mormonism, one must decide whether they believe the Bible is true. Is the Bible God's inspired Word? Is the Bible unique to all other books? The Bible itself tells us that it contains the truth, without any mixture of error.

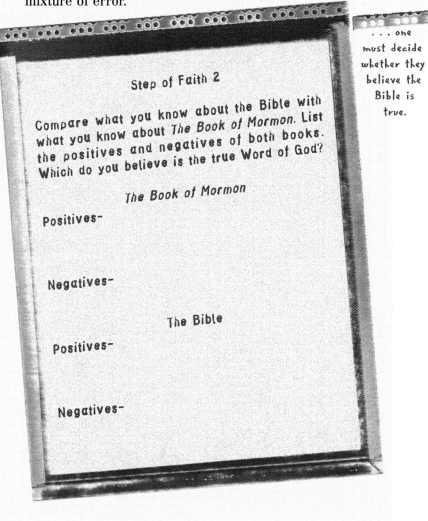

Step of Faith 2

Compare what you know about the Bible with what you know about *The Book of Mormon*. List the positives and negatives of both books. Which do you believe is the true Word of God?

The Book of Mormon

Positives—

Negatives—

The Bible

Positives—

Negatives—

... one must decide whether they believe the Bible is true.

WHAT MORMONS BELIEVE ABOUT GOD

As Christians, we believe there is only one true God who exists in three persons (God the Father, God the Son, and God the Holy Spirit). Mormons believe the Father, Son, and the Holy Ghost are three separate and distinct Gods. Mormons will also say there are many gods throughout the universe and that every Mormon who is "exalted" will himself become a god some day.

When Mormonism teaches there are many gods, and that we can become one, it denies what God Himself teaches in His Word.

This is clearly not the teaching of the Bible. God Himself says, *Before me no god was formed, nor will there be one after me (Isa. 43:10)*. Also, God declares, *I am the Lord, and there is no other;*

apart from me there is no God (Isa. 45:5) When Mormonism teaches that there are many gods and that we can become one, it denies what God Himself teaches in His Word.

WHAT MORMONS BELIEVE ABOUT JESUS

All Mormons will say they believe in the true, biblical Jesus Christ. During the Christmas holidays a nativity scene will probably be displayed on the lawn of their churches. This can be very confusing for some Christians. Do they really believe in Jesus the same way Christians do?

Mormonism teaches that Jesus is the spirit-brother of Satan, and was the Son of a Heavenly Father and a Heavenly Mother in the preexistence. However, the Bible says that *In the beginning was the Word, and the Word was with God, and the Word was God (John 1:1)* and *The Word became flesh and made his dwelling among us. We have seen his glory, the glory of the One and Only, who came from the Father, full of grace and truth. (John 1:14).*

In Mormon teaching, Jesus is special only because He was the first child born. But He was only one of many gods who earned His salvation, immortality, and godhood. So, Mormons believe that Jesus Christ is not unique. Since Mormons believe every "exalted" man will one day become a god, we can all become like Jesus and experience the same Godhood.

If we believe the Bible, we know all of this to be false. Jesus Christ is God. He is not the brother of the devil. In fact, He came to destroy the works of the devil. *First John 3:8b* says, *The reason the Son of God appeared was to destroy the devil's work.* Jesus is unique to all others.

Since Mormons believe every "exalted" man will one day become a god, we can all become like Jesus and experience the same Godhood.

15

"I do believe in Jesus Christ. My church is even called the Church of Jesus Christ of Latter-day Saints!" Melody replied.

"I understand that. But by what you said, you also think Jesus was just another god," Todd said quickly.

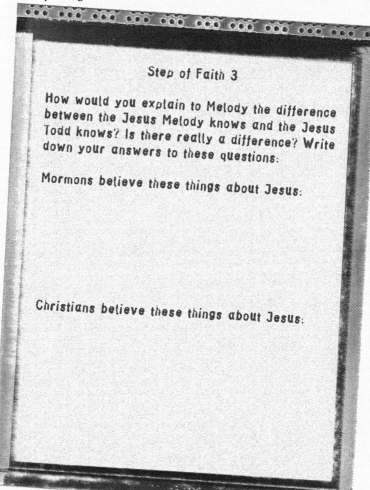

Step of Faith 3

How would you explain to Melody the difference between the Jesus Melody knows and the Jesus Todd knows? Is there really a difference? Write down your answers to these questions:

Mormons believe these things about Jesus:

Christians believe these things about Jesus:

Mormonism teaches that Jesus is the spirit-brother of Satan.

"So, explain what's wrong with that!" Melody replied, then glared at Todd waiting for an answer.

Todd knew he couldn't give up, even if Melody might not like what he had to say.

WHAT MORMONS BELIEVE ABOUT JESUS' DEATH ON THE CROSS

Mormons claim that salvation comes because of "the atonement." However, the Mormon church does not believe in biblical reconciliation – or being made right with God through Jesus Christ – but reconciliation by its own means. The value of the atonement in Mormon thinking is that it gives people the opportunity to earn their own salvation through good works.

Mormons believe that Jesus died on the cross in order to bring about the resurrection of the dead for all people. So Mormons are grateful for Jesus' death only because they can now be raised from the dead. In other words, they do not think Christ's death had the power to purchase full salvation for anyone.

The Bible, however, says that Christ's death on the cross actually paid the penalty for all sin. Any person can now believe in Jesus Christ as Lord and be reconciled to God. *They replied, "Believe in the Lord Jesus, and you will be saved – you and your household" (Acts 16:31).* Another Scripture says, *For what I received I passed on to you as of first importance: that Christ died for our sins according to the Scriptures, that he was buried, that he was raised on the third day according to the Scriptures (1 Cor. 15:3-4).*

In essence, Mormonism completely disagrees with the saving value of Christ's death on the cross. Instead, it tells people that their good works

The value of the atonement in Mormon thinking is that it gives people the opportunity to earn their own salvation through good works.

will save them, forgive them of their sins, and eventually send them to heaven.

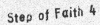

Step of Faith 4

Read *Ephesians 1:7* and answer the following questions.

What does *redemption through his blood* mean?

Who can forgive our sins?

What are the *riches of God's grace*?

WHAT MORMONS BELIEVE ABOUT SALVATION AND LIFE AFTER DEATH

Mormonism teaches that everyone must earn their salvation by works. This belief totally disagrees

19

with what the Bible teaches. *For it is by grace you have been saved, through faith – and this not from yourselves, it is the gift of God – not by works, so that no one can boast (Eph. 2:8-9).* Mormon teaching on salvation also presents different kinds of salvation leading to different kinds of heaven.

First, there is general salvation called "salvation by grace." Anyone can have this form of salvation. It basically makes a person immortal.

Second, there is individual salvation. Individual salvation determines which of the three heavens one will go to and whether or not one earns Godhood. Individual salvation is based on a person's good works. The "kingdom of glory" or heaven one goes to depends on the kinds of good works a person has performed.

Individual salvation determines which of the three heavens one will go to and whether or not one earns Godhood.

The lowest kingdom of glory is called the telestial kingdom. It is the place of the wicked, where almost everyone will go. Mormon doctrine teaches that people who go to the telestial kingdom will be excluded from the immediate presence of God, although He will be present with them in some indirect way.

The kingdom above the telestial kingdom is called the terrestrial kingdom of glory. This is where lukewarm Mormons and good non-Mormons will go after death. However, Mormons believe that even after death, one can still go to the highest level of heaven (the celestial kingdom) if someone is baptized and performs temple ordinances on their behalf in a Mormon temple.

The highest kingdom of glory is the celestial kingdom. Mormons believe that a person will go to this kingdom by being completely obedient to Mormon teachings and theology. This kingdom also allows a person to progress toward becoming a god and reproducing themselves forever. For women, this means they will have the ability and desire to be eternally pregnant!

Step of Faith 5

There is a big difference between what Christians and Mormons believe about salvation and life after death! Write a "C" in the blank beside each statement that is a Christian belief. Write an "M" in the blank if it is a Mormon belief.

_____ Three kingdoms of glory.

_____ Everyone will receive salvation.

_____ Salvation comes through Jesus Christ alone.

_____ We can become gods when we die.

_____ Salvation by grace.

_____ Salvation by works and good deeds.

_____ Everyone in heaven will be united with God.

_____ General salvation or "salvation by grace."

WHAT MORMONS BELIEVE ABOUT THEIR CHURCH

Baptists believe they are one of several Christian denominations. Mormons, however, do not claim

Mormons, however, do not claim to be merely one part of the Christian religion. From their earliest days, they have claimed to be the true church.

to be merely one part of the Christian religion. From their earliest days, they have claimed to be the true church. Mormons believe that others,

22

even if they claim to be Christians, do not possess "the fullness of the gospel" and thus cannot receive exaltation in the celestial kingdom.

The Church of Jesus Christ of Latter-day Saints is very powerful and influential. They currently have a membership of over 8.5 million people

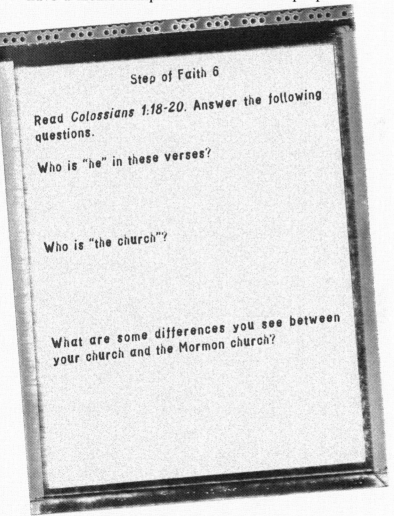

worldwide, with over 49,000 missionaries. It is one of the largest non-Christian religions in our country originating in the last 200 years.

WHERE DO YOU GO FROM HERE?

"So, what happened?" Kristi asked with eyes wide with anticipation.

"We talked for a pretty long time. She got really mad at me for a while," Todd answered as he looked down at the ground and kicked a rock near his foot.

"Well, does she understand? Did she accept Christ?" Heather asked.

"No," Todd said, and shook his head in disappointment. "She said she wanted to think about it. She said her whole family is Mormon. She doesn't know what they would do if she suddenly said she was a Christian. Her family thinks they are Christians already."

"Well, at least you tried. I didn't even try to talk to her," said Kristi.

As the three walked along in silence, Heather suddenly had an idea.

"Hey, Todd, what if I talk to Melody later and invite her to our church after camp is over? Maybe if Melody keeps hearing the truth, she will understand."

"Great idea, Heather! Right now I think we just need to be her friend. . . that's the only way we're going to get her to listen to us."

"And we need to listen to her. Melody probably has a lot of questions."

Right now I think we just need to be her friend. . . that's the only way we're going to get her to listen to us."

Step of Faith 7

List some ways you can be a friend to someone who is a Mormon or non-Christian. What are some ways you can share your faith?

1.

2.

3.

4.

5.

"I can't believe you asked that Ryan guy to come with us to the football game!"

CHAPTER 2

JEHOVAH'S WITNESSES: ARE THEY KNOCKING ON YOUR DOOR?

"I was so embarrassed during the national anthem. He just sat there!"

"I'm going to get some popcorn. Anybody else want something?" asked Kristi.
"I do! Here's some money," said Todd, handing her a five-dollar bill. Heather laughed at Todd's remark.
Kristi jokingly glared at Todd. "I think you should go with me," she said.
Todd and Heather got up and slid their way down through the crowd in the bleachers.
There was a roar from the crowd as the home team made a great defensive play.
"I can't believe you asked that Ryan guy to come with us to the football game!" Kristi spouted, suddenly becoming serious. "I was so embarrassed during the national anthem. He just sat there! Did you notice the way everyone started looking at

27

him? And Ryan didn't even care!"

"He doesn't believe in singing the national anthem or pledging allegiance to the flag or any of that kind of stuff," Todd replied.

"He could have at least stood up!" said Kristi, as they walked up to the concession line. "And what do you mean when you say that he doesn't believe in that kind of stuff?"

"Ryan is a Jehovah's Witness. I was lucky to get him to even come to the game. His parents hardly ever let him do ANY school activities," Todd stated.

Kristi grabbed her popcorn and drink and turned to Todd, "Well, is he going to do anything else weird that I should be aware of?"

"I don't think so. Just try and be nice to him, Kristi. It has taken me a month of talking to him in English class just to get him to do anything outside of school."

"Okay, I'll try. I just wish I knew what to expect. I've never been around a Jehovah's Witness before!"

Jehovah's Witnesses have some really distinct beliefs which set them apart from other religions.

How would you react to meeting a Jehovah's Witness? Most of the time, the only way we recognize someone as a Jehovah's Witness is when they come knocking on our door selling Watchtower literature. Jehovah's Witnesses have some really distinct beliefs which set them apart from other religions.

Many of their beliefs are extremely different from Christianity. With a name like Jehovah's Witnesses, they sound very Christian. Jehovah is a name for God, and witnesses are what we are to be for Christ. But, are they Christians? Look at several basic Jehovah's Witness beliefs and decide for yourself.

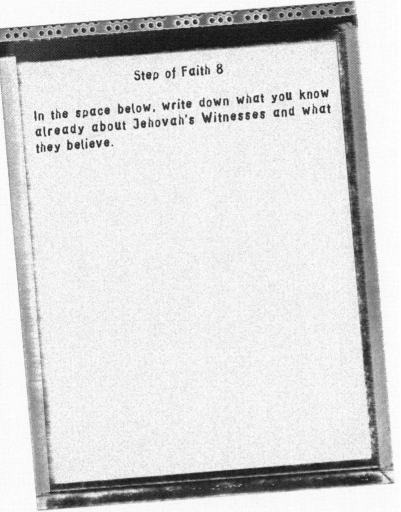

WHO ARE THE JEHOVAH'S WITNESSES?

The Jehovah's Witnesses are a religious sect begun by Charles Taze Russell in the 1870s. To formulate their beliefs, Russell looked at the teachings of Second Adventists, Christadelphianism, and his own beliefs about the Bible.

The leaders of the Jehovah's Witnesses are a group of men who head an organization called the Watchtower Bible and Tract Society. This small group has absolute spiritual authority over the nearly five million members.

The Watchtower Society is headed by a president, and in recent decades, each of the five presidents has claimed that God Himself was the source and author of their interpretations of the Bible and doctrines. Interestingly, each president has interpreted the Bible differently from (and sometimes even in contradiction to) the others.

Interestingly, each president has interpreted the Bible differently from (and sometimes even in contradiction to) the others.

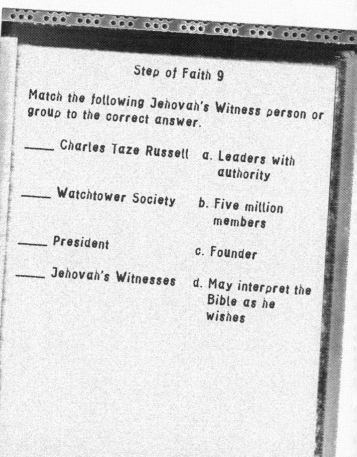

Step of Faith 9

Match the following Jehovah's Witness person or group to the correct answer.

____ Charles Taze Russell   a. Leaders with authority

____ Watchtower Society   b. Five million members

____ President   c. Founder

____ Jehovah's Witnesses   d. May interpret the Bible as he wishes

WHAT ATTRACTS PEOPLE TO THE JEHOVAH'S WITNESSES?

Many people are attracted to the Jehovah's Witnesses because they claim to have the answers to life's problems. They claim to be able to offer divine guidance to their members. Also, they stress positive moral and family values.

The Watchtower Society attracts people who are looking for answers or who are frightened about the future. The Witnesses are very dedicated and committed to their beliefs. They devote much time and effort to help others understand their Bible, *The New World Translation of the Holy Scriptures.*

Step of Faith 10

List some of life's problems which you think Jehovah's Witnesses try to answer. Beside each problem, write a Scripture reference from the Bible that could give hope to someone with that problem.

PROBLEM SCRIPTURE

1.

2.

3.

4.

5.

31

WHAT THEY BELIEVE ABOUT GOD

Jehovah's Witnesses believe there is one true God, Jehovah. They teach that God is only one person. They do not believe that God existed in human form through Jesus. Also, they do not believe that the Holy Spirit is part of God, but totally separate and impersonal. Jehovah's Witnesses reject the Bible's teaching about the one true God existing as three persons. The idea of the Trinity is unreasonable to them. To Jehovah's Witnesses, the God that Christians believe in is some kind of strange three-headed God!

Instead, Christians believe the Bible teaches that the one true God exists eternally as three persons – God the Father, Jesus Christ, and the Holy Spirit.

They do not believe that God existed in human form through Jesus.

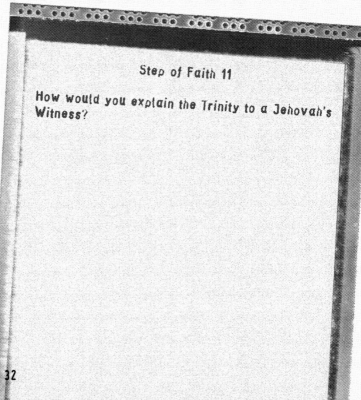

Step of Faith 11

How would you explain the Trinity to a Jehovah's Witness?

WHAT THEY BELIEVE ABOUT JESUS

Jehovah's Witnesses teach that Jesus Christ was the first creation of God. They believe that the angel Michael, who came along later, was then changed into the human form of Jesus. When Jesus died, He was changed into an improved and immortal version of the angel Michael. So, Jesus and the angel Michael are one in the same. This is all very confusing!

Jehovah's Witnesses also do not believe that Jesus died on the cross. They think He died on a torture stake. Members of the Jehovah's Witnesses think the cross is a pagan symbol. Jehovah's Witnesses do not believe that people saw Jesus' physical body after His resurrection. Instead, they believe that He was in the form of a spirit.

Jehovah's Witnesses also do not believe that Jesus died on the cross. They think He died on a torture stake.

"I thought you said he wouldn't do anything else weird!"

Todd could see Kristi's anger as her face began to turn red. He searched for an answer, then finally said, "Well, I didn't think he would. I'm sorry, Kristi!"

"It just wasn't fair! I'm here to watch a football game, not to explain why I wear a cross necklace."

"I know you were embarrassed," Todd apologized, "and none of us really tried to help you explain."

"Was embarrassed?! I still am! He said my cross was pagan!" Heather paused, "And I didn't do a very good job explaining why I wear it."

"You did the best you could, Kristi. I mean, you were put on the spot in the middle of a ball game with several people trying to listen to you."

Kristi sighed. "I still wish I could have done a better job of explaining it," she replied.

Members of the Jehovah's Witnesses think the cross is a pagan symbol.

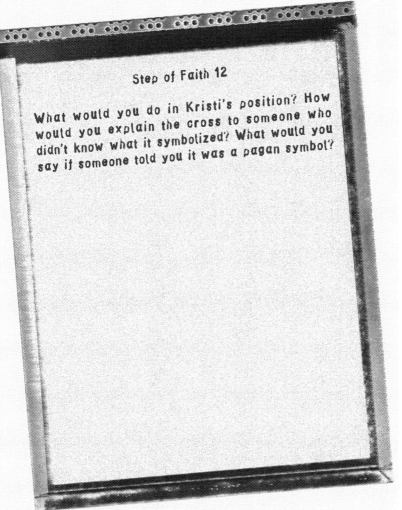

WHAT THEY BELIEVE ABOUT SALVATION AND LIFE AFTER DEATH

Jehovah's Witnesses believe that there are different classes of people who will be saved by good works. Each class is working to gain a different salvation.

The first class is made up of a small group of

144,000 people called "the Anointed." These people are elected by God for special spiritual privileges. This class receives special blessings and the privilege of being born again. However, these special blessings can be taken away at any time if the person is disobedient.

Jehovah's Witnesses also believe that being born again is being water baptized and anointed by God so they can be recreated by God as a spirit creature after death. This is the same idea as God supposedly recreating Jesus into the angel Michael after His death. Jehovah's Witnesses teach that Jesus was born again at His baptism. The 144,000 are the spiritually privileged who will eventually be recreated like Jesus, and will rule with Him in heaven.

The second class is called the "other sheep." They do not receive any special blessings and cannot be born again. The average Jehovah's Witness would fall into this category. At death God does not recreate these people into spirit beings, but recreates their physical bodies to live only on the earth. These people are told they will be ruled over by Jesus (Michael) and the 144,000 in heaven.

It should be added that non-Jehovah's Witnesses who have lived a good life can earn salvation after death. If they are granted a second chance, they may become "other sheep." They will be recreated by Jehovah to live for 1,000 years. They may also live beyond this 1,000 years if they live perfectly during this time.

The 144,000 are the spiritually privileged who will eventually be recreated like Jesus, and will rule with Him in heaven.

> **Step of Faith 13**
>
> Fill in the blanks below about what Jehovah's Witnesses believe about salvation and life after death.
>
> 1. Jehovah's Witnesses believe people are saved by _____.
> 2. There are _____ classes of people who will be saved.
> 3. The first class is a small group of 144,000 people known as "_____."
> 4. The first class is elected by God for _____.
> 5. Also, the first class can be _____ again.
> 6. The second class is called the "_____."
> 7. The second class can only live on the _____.
> 8. Non-Jehovah's Witnesses may earn salvation after _____.

THE NEW WORLD TRANSLATION: IS IT ACCURATE?

Jehovah's Witnesses believe that the Bible is the final source of authority. However, the Watchtower Society claims that the *New World Translation* is the most accurate or one of the most accurate

translations of the Bible yet produced. It was translated during the 1950s by seven men. In it, hundreds of verses have been changed to match the Jehovah's Witness beliefs. In fact, this version of the Bible is rewritten every few years with additional changes to bring it into closer agreement with the religion's teachings.

The Watchtower Society believes *The New World Translation* is accurate, reliable, and a faithful translation of God's Word. They believe that God Himself supervised its translation by angels who controlled the translators. Again, Jehovah's Witnesses believe the Watchtower Society is God's sole channel for communicating His will, so they believe *The New World Translation* is correct.

This version of the Bible is rewritten every few years with additional changes to bring it into closer agreement with the religion's teachings.

A few of the many changes include that Jesus was nailed to an upright pole without a crossbeam. *The New World Translation of the Holy Scriptures* has taken the cross out of the New Testament and replaced it with the torture stake. Also, since the Holy Spirit is not considered God, the words *Holy Spirit* are never capitalized in this translation. The Holy Spirit is referred to as "holy spirit" or "active force." The Bible of Jehovah's Witnesses also attempts to remove all evidence of Jesus' deity. *The New World Translation of the Holy Scriptures* also inserts the word *Jehovah* 237 times in the New Testament.

There have been many, many changes to the Jehovah's Witnesses' Bible. Surprisingly, Jehovah's Witnesses openly admit that the Watchtower Society continually revises *The New World Translation of the Holy Scriptures*. With change after change, how can it really be the accurate Word of God?

39

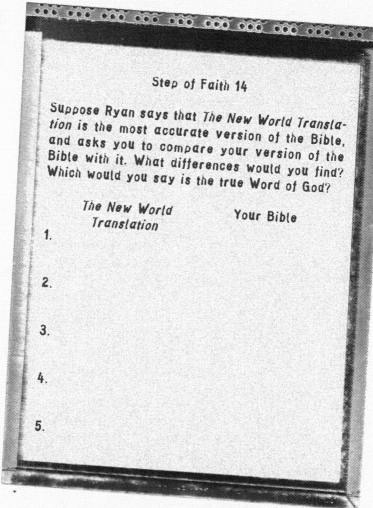

THE KINGDOM HALL

The Kingdom Hall is a busy place. Jehovah's Witnesses meet there four times a week. A fifth meeting is held each week in a home. The main focus of this meeting is Bible study (using *The New World Translation of the Holy Scriptures*) and training in how to use the materials published by the Watchtower Society.

The Kingdom Hall is also the place where "publishers" are trained on how to answer questions and convert the world. Publishers are the volunteers who go door to door and sell Watchtower publications. Publications which a Witness will try to sell you include *The New World Translation of the Holy Scriptures*, *The Watchtower*, and *Awake!* magazines. Witnesses who knock on your door are trained to tell you about their beliefs and invite you to Bible studies at the Kingdom Hall. Publishers are expected to spend at least 10 hours a month knocking on doors selling literature. Jehovah's Witnesses are zealous in their outreach because of their belief that the end of the world is near. They give long hours to their ministry. They believe their efforts will result in their salvation.

Witnesses who knock on your door are trained to tell you about their beliefs and invite you to Bible studies at the Kingdom Hall.

Step of Faith 15

How will you respond the next time a publisher from the Jehovah's Witnesses knocks on your door? What proof can you give them for Christianity?

41

They believe that governments are part of the Satanic order. As a result, they do not vote, salute, pledge allegiance to any flag, or sing national anthems.

Since they think the world is about to end, Jehovah's Witnesses shun "worldly" events. Their children are not encouraged to be involved in extra-curricular activities at school. Also, they are not encouraged to attend college. They believe that governments are part of the Satanic order. As a result, they do not vote, salute, pledge allegiance to any flag, or sing national anthems. They also do not celebrate Christmas or Easter.

"Hey Ryan, thanks for coming with me to the game," Todd said as they left the stadium.

"I had a good time. I don't usually make it to the games," Ryan said in reply.

"Maybe you can go with us to the game next weekend. We're playing our big rival!"

"Well, I don't know. I'll have to see what my parents say. They're pretty strict when it comes to my activities," Ryan explained.

"Well, if you can't make it to the game, we'll try to do something else next weekend. Okay?"

"Sure, that would be great!"

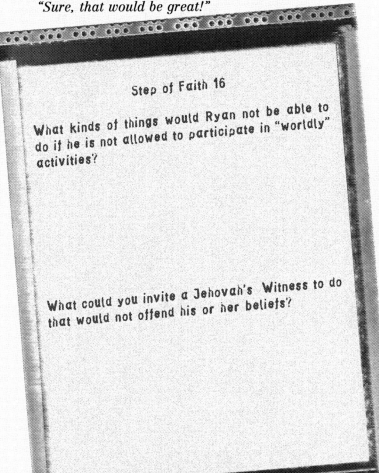

Step of Faith 16

What kinds of things would Ryan not be able to do if he is not allowed to participate in "worldly" activities?

What could you invite a Jehovah's Witness to do that would not offend his or her beliefs?

CHAPTER 3
MUSLIMS: WHY ARE THEY SO MYSTERIOUS?

For many Christians, Muslims are a mysterious people.

"What is he doing?!"

"I think he's praying, Kristi, but you don't have to keep staring at him like that," Todd answered.

"But look how he just sits there on his knees without moving. Are you sure he's OK? Watch him!" Kristi stated, and continued to stare at the other student.

"Oh, Kristi," Heather spoke up. "That's the way Muslims pray. He prays like that every day at noon."

Todd looked at Heather and asked, "How do you know he's a Muslim?"

"You haven't met Ali? He's a foreign exchange student from Saudi Arabia. He's been here for about a month," Heather explained, then rolled her eyes jokingly at Kristi and Todd. "Where have you guys been?!"

"I can't believe I've never noticed him praying at lunch before," Todd mentioned as he shook his head.

"Yeah, I know I would remember it if I had ever seen him doing this!" Kristi commented as she

45

continued to watch the new student.

"Ali is in my chemistry class. He's a nice, quiet guy. Usually, there are more people out here eating lunch and so you don't even notice it when he goes over there and starts praying like that," Heather said.

"So, what has he told you about being a Muslim? What does he believe?" Todd questioned Heather.

"He hasn't talked to me that much. I'm not really sure what he believes. All I know is that whatever he believes, he believes in it very strongly!" Heather replied as she looked over at Ali again. "I mean, who would have the guts to pray like that in front of the whole school?"

"Yeah, he must be devoted to his religion," Kristi remarked. "I would never pray like that in front of everyone!"

"I wish I knew more about Muslims and what they believe," Todd said thoughtfully. "I only know that their beliefs are totally different from Christians."

"Yeah, how can we ever reach someone like Ali? We don't know anything about his beliefs or his way of life," Heather added.

Muslims not only have a religion that is quite different from Christianity, they have an entirely different way of life!

For most Christians, Muslims are a mysterious people. They talk about the one and only true God, Allah. They pray five times a day. Because many Muslim people are from Arab countries, they often dress differently. The ladies usually wear veils. The men may have up to four wives. Muslims not only have a religion that is quite different from Christianity, they have an entirely different way of life!

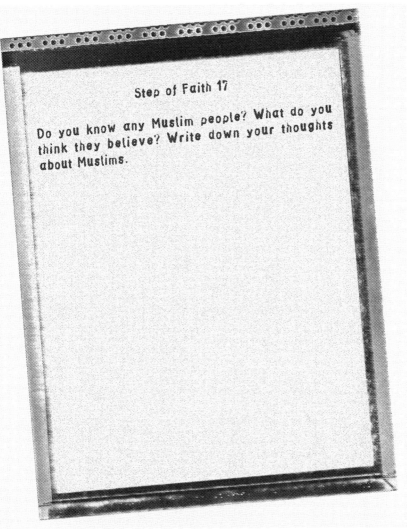

Step of Faith 17

Do you know any Muslim people? What do you think they believe? Write down your thoughts about Muslims.

WHO ARE THE MUSLIMS AND MUHAMMAD?

It is said that in the year 610, Muhammad was resting in a cave when he heard a voice. He was very frightened at first, but soon realized that he had been chosen by Allah, the God of Islam, to be his messenger. Muhammad's concept of Allah and

Islam attempts to regulate every part of the Muslim's life.

his idea that he was a prophet came partially from his understanding of the beliefs of Jews and Christians.

Muhammad considered himself a prophet in the Judeo-Christian tradition. He spoke about many biblical characters: Adam, Noah, Abraham, Moses, the children of Israel, Mary, and even Jesus. He spoke against idolatry and preached about the one living Allah. Muhammad believed Allah was interested not only in Jews and Christians, but also the Arabs. This was the beginning of the Muslim people.

Muslims, or Moslems as they are sometimes called, are believers and followers of Islam. Islam is not only a religion, but it is also a way of life. The word *Islam* comes from a word which means *submission to God.* The Muslim people believe that perfect peace comes when one's life is totally surrendered to God.

Islam attempts to regulate every part of the Muslim's life. Islam sets up spiritual goals for the people, as well as laws and institutions. Little is left for the individual person to decide.

Islam tells its people when to pray, how to pray, how many times a day to pray, and even what direction to face when they are praying. Also, there are many laws about marriage, divorce, property, and inheritance. Islam also has specific rules about war as well as how to maintain peace. The Muslim people are very specific about what is right and wrong.

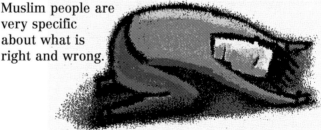

48

Step of Faith 18

Mark the following statements true or false:

_____ 1. Moslem and Muslim both mean the same thing.

_____ 2. Muhammad spoke about Noah, Abraham, Jesus, and others in the Old and New Testaments.

_____ 3. Allah was the prophet of Muhammad.

_____ 4. Islam comes from a word which means submission to God.

_____ 5. The laws of Islam leave many decisions to the people.

_____ 6. Muhammad did not consider himself to be a prophet.

_____ 7. Muhammad heard a voice telling him that he was to be Allah's messenger.

WHO IS THEIR GOD?

To become a Muslim, one has to repeat this statement of belief: "There is no deity but Allah, and Muhammad is the messenger of Allah." Muhammad proclaimed Allah to be the one and only true God. Muslims believe Allah is all-seeking, all-knowing, and all-powerful. The Muslim people stress the power of Allah more than anything else. Muslims believe Allah (which means "the God") created the world. After creating the world, Allah created man.

Allah is everything to the people of Islam. He is the supreme creator, lawgiver, judge, sustainer, provider, and ordainer. They reject the Christian belief in the trinity of God. The idea that Allah might have a partner is considered to be an unforgivable sin.

WHAT ABOUT JESUS?

Muslims think Allah took Jesus to heaven before the crucifixion and there was no resurrection.

According to Muslims, Jesus was only one of many great prophets. In fact, they place Jesus in the same category as Abraham, Noah, Jonah, and other prophets mentioned in the Old Testament. However, Jesus is not as important as Muhammad when Muslims rank the prophets.

Muslims do not believe that Jesus was the son of God. They also do not accept the belief that Jesus lived a sinless life. Since Muslims believe that everyone is born innocently – without a sin nature – there was no need for Jesus to die on the cross. Instead, they believe that Judas was placed on the cross in Jesus' place and that Allah took Jesus to heaven before the crucifixion. So, Muslims do not believe in Jesus' death, burial, or resurrection.

We know that these Muslim beliefs are in direct opposition to what the Bible says. The books of *Matthew, Mark, Luke,* and *John* all have accounts of Jesus' death, burial, and resurrection.

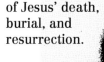

50

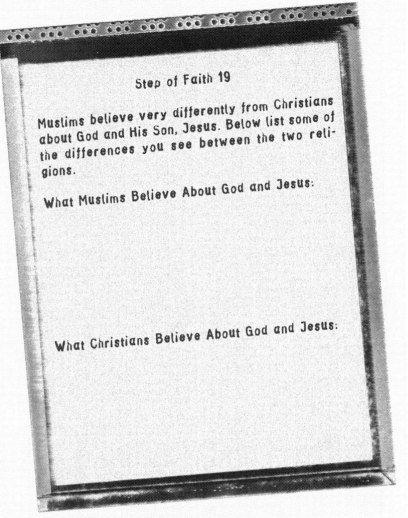

WHAT HAPPENS AFTER DEATH?
Muslims believe in both heaven and hell, but their view is very different from the Christian view.

Even though Muslims believe that all people are born without sin, they also believe that every person will be judged according to the good works they have done. So, Muslims must earn their

> There is no assurance for Muslims that they will go to heaven; only Allah knows who will be rewarded.

salvation and admittance into heaven. If one is loyal and obedient to Muslim teachings, he will be rewarded with heaven.

For Muslims, sin is doing anything that Allah has said they are not to do, or failing to do anything that Allah has commanded them to do. Muslims take sin very seriously. They believe that those who follow Allah's commands will go to the Islamic heaven. Those who do not will be tormented in hell. There is no assurance for Muslims that they will go to heaven; only Allah knows who will be rewarded.

Islamic heaven, called Paradise, is a place of pleasure. Men who are allowed to go to heaven will recline on soft couches and be served wine by the maidens there. The men may marry as many of the maidens as they wish. If a person is not admitted to heaven, he goes to hell. Muslims are constantly wanting to know what they can do in order to go to heaven.

"Wow! I can't believe Ali thinks that!" Todd exclaimed.

"I know! How can I explain it to him so that he understands? I mean, how would you feel if you thought you had to work hard at doing all the right things all your life. . . and still didn't know if you would go to heaven?" Heather asked, then waited for Todd's answer.

But all Todd could do was shake his head and wonder.

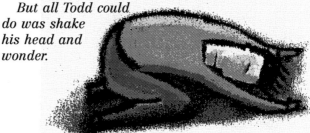

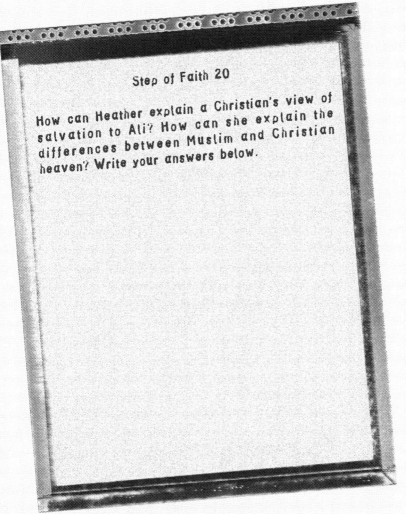

Step of Faith 20

How can Heather explain a Christian's view of salvation to Ali? How can she explain the differences between Muslim and Christian heaven? Write your answers below.

THE BIBLE OR THE KORAN?

Muslims believe in four sacred books written by Allah and revealed to prophets: the Torah, revealed to Moses; the Zabur, Psalms of David; the Injil, the gospel of Jesus; and the *Koran* (or *Qu'ran)*, which is believed to be Allah's final word to mankind.

Muslims believe the earlier revealed books have been corrupted by Jews and Christians. Therefore, the Koran overrules all the other writings.

Arabs trace their ancestry back to Ishmael, the son of Abraham *(Gen. 16:15)*. When Abraham and Sarah did not have children, Sarah suggested that Abraham take her maid, Hagar, and have a child with her. So Hagar had Abraham's son, Ishmael. Later, Sarah had Abraham's son, Isaac. Sarah then had Hagar and Ishmael banished from the tribe. According to the *Koran,* Ishmael goes to the city of Mecca. His descendants, growing up in Arabia, are Muslims. The descendants of Isaac, they believe, are Jews.

The Koran is as important to the Muslim as Jesus and the Bible are to the Christian.

Although the Bible did have great influence on the teachings of the Islamic religion, the Islamic religion actually revolves around the *Koran*. The *Koran* is as important to the Muslim as Jesus and the Bible are to the Christian. Muslim children begin to memorize the *Koran* at an early age. The *Koran* may be the most memorized book in the world.

Interestingly, the Bible also influenced the writings in the *Koran*. Muhammad was unable to read the Scriptures, but he was able to learn many Old Testament stories from Jewish friends. Muhammad then repeated these stories in the *Koran*. The *Koran* could be described as a mixture of Jewish legends and Old Testament Scriptures from the Bible.

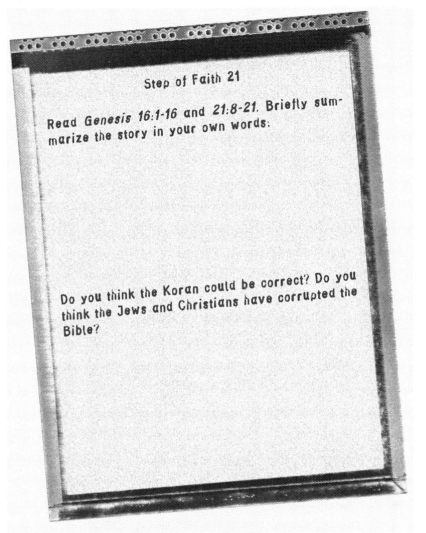

THE PRACTICING MUSLIM

There are certain things which Muslims must practice to demonstrate their faith. Every Muslim must make a profession of faith and bear witness to his beliefs. The creed of Islam says: "There is no deity but Allah, and Muhammad is the messenger of Allah." This is the most often repeated sentence in the Islamic world. Saying this one sentence admits a person into the religion.

A Muslim also prays five times a day. The prayer must be in Arabic and the person must face the city of Mecca when he or she prays. A person is allowed to pray anywhere. In addition to praying, Muslims give two and a half percent of their annual wealth to the Islamic community.

Fasting is expected of Muslims during the month of Ramadan. Ramadan is the ninth month of the Muslim calendar, and is the holy month for Muslims throughout the world. The fasting begins at dawn, usually after a meal, and ends at sunset. This fasting continues for 28 consecutive days. During Ramadan, the nights are spent praying and reading the *Koran*.

In addition to fasting, Muslims are encouraged and expected to go to Mecca at least once during their lifetimes. Hundreds of thousands of Muslims from all parts of the world make this pilgrimage every year.

Lastly, the *Koran* has many references to war and the Muslim's duty to fight. Many Muslims believe "holy effort" or a "holy conquest" in the name of Allah is both an inner spiritual struggle and an outer struggle to defend the faith. The concept of "holy efforts," they believe, will be used to conquer others for Allah.

Every Muslim must make a profession of faith and bear witness to his beliefs.

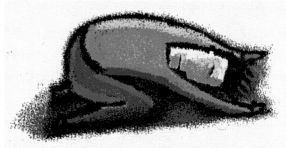

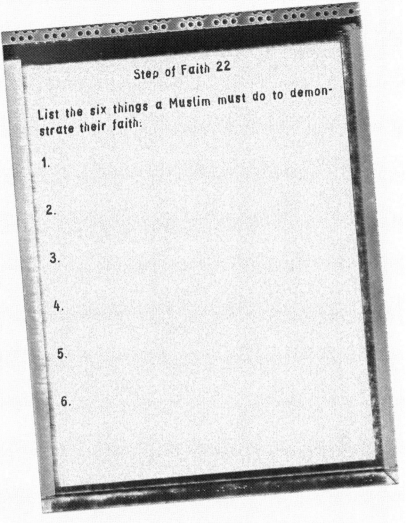

DO MUSLIMS HAVE CHURCHES?

The basic duty in Muslim worship is to be together in the brotherhood of Islam. They do not have pastors or priests that lead the people in worship. Instead, the most respected leaders are the scholars who study the *Koran*. Any Muslim has the right to lead prayers and teach others. The religious leaders who do perform marriages, funerals, and sometimes preach are called imams.

The only form of church that Muslims have is meeting in mosques for prayer. Most of the prayers in mosques are performed individually. There is no such thing as membership in a mosque. Although there is no day more special than any other, Friday at noon is when most Muslims get together for corporate prayers.

Step of Faith 23

How is your church different from a Muslim mosque? What kind of activities happen at your church?

CAN YOU SHARE CHRIST WITH A MUSLIM?

"I can't believe Ali is going to meet with us!" Todd said as he grabbed his Bible out of his locker.

"Okay, now we've agreed to help each other out, right?" Heather questioned.

"Right," Todd quickly replied.

Heather paused for a moment, then sighed, "I just hope we can find all the verses we need. I really want Ali to understand who Jesus is, and this may be our only chance to talk with him about it."

"I know what you mean. But don't worry; God will help us. Let's go. Ali's waiting over there," Todd nodded toward a tree on the school lawn.

Heather and Todd prayed together, then started walking towards Ali.

The only form of church that Muslims have is meeting in mosques for prayer.

Step of Faith 24

If you went with Todd and Heather to share Christ with Ali, what would you say? Where would you start?

Below list verses of the Bible to back up your Christian beliefs.

CHAPTER 4
BUDDHISTS: A RELIGION WITH NO GOD

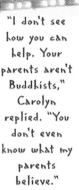

"I don't see how you can help. Your parents aren't Buddhists," Carolyn replied. "You don't even know what my parents believe."

"Nobody understands what it's like!" Carolyn exclaimed. "I can't believe I even made it to youth group tonight. They hate that I come to church every week. They think my becoming a Christian was some kind of peer pressure thing."

"Well, maybe we don't understand exactly what you're going through, but we can still try to help," whispered Heather.

"I don't see how you can help. Your parents aren't Buddhists," Carolyn replied. "You don't even know what my parents believe."

"Carolyn, what if you tell us some of what they believe? We can help you compare it with what we believe as Christians. Maybe that will help you explain to them why you became a Christian."

"Yeah, it wouldn't hurt us to learn a little about Buddhism. It would really help us the next time we come over to your house and are talking with your parents," Kristi replied.

"I know I don't know anything about Buddhism," Todd said, starting to laugh, "except that they have statues of that guy with the big stomach."

61

"Don't laugh! We have one at our house. You know, maybe if I can explain better why I accepted Jesus as my Lord and Savior, then they will quit giving me such a hard time about wanting to come to youth group and church," Carolyn said with a hopeful sigh.

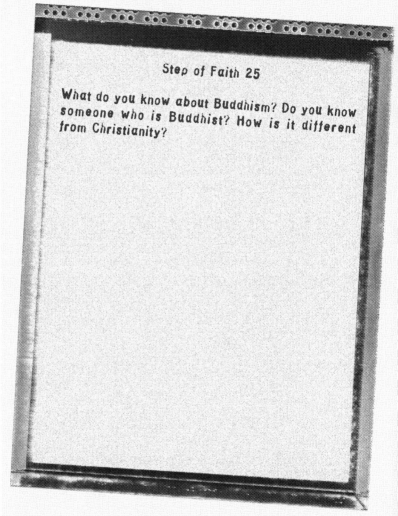

Step of Faith 25

What do you know about Buddhism? Do you know someone who is Buddhist? How is it different from Christianity?

WHERE DID BUDDHA COME FROM?

Siddhartha Gautama of the Sakyas was born around 560 B.C. in Northern India. His father was a king, so Siddhartha was surrounded with every good thing life had to offer. The king made sure the prince saw none of the ugliness of the world. Specifically, the prince was to be guarded from contact with sickness, suffering, and death. Even when the prince went out riding, the road was to be cleared of these sights.

One day, however, a decrepit old man was overlooked. That day, the prince learned the fact of old age. Later, on another ride, Siddhartha encountered a sick man by the road; and on another journey, a corpse. Finally, on a fourth ride, he saw a monk. On that day he learned the possibility of withdrawal from the world. All of these things had a great influence on Siddhartha. Once the prince realized the certainty of bodily pain, he could not return to his life of fleshly pleasure.

Buddha means the enlightened or awakened one.

One night, at the age of 29, he made the break from the world. This is called his "Great Going Forth." He left while his wife and son slept and rode off on his horse. The prince cut his hair, put on hunter's clothes, and went into the forest in search of enlightenment.

During his six years in the forest, Siddhartha learned from two masters. He accepted Hindu wisdom, traditions, and philosophy. This is when he began being called Buddha. Buddha means *the enlightened* or *awakened one*.

At the end of his time in the forest, it is believed that Buddha then traveled the paths of India for approximately 44 years. During this time, he founded an order of monks. He had no home of his own. Only during the rainy season did he spend any length of time in one place.

Many people then began to follow the teachings of Buddha. Even today many people look to the writing of the Buddha for wisdom and the answers to life's problems.

Step of Faith 26

Answer the following questions true or false.

____ 1. Siddhartha was born a wealthy prince.

____ 2. The king let Siddhartha experience everything the world had to offer.

____ 3. When he saw suffering, disease, death, and a monk, it changed Siddhartha's life forever.

____ 4. The Great Going Forth was Siddhartha's break from the world.

____ 5. Siddhartha went to a great city in search of enlightenment.

____ 6. Siddhartha became known as Buddha, which means enlightened or awakened one.

____ 7. Today, only a few people follow the teachings of Buddha.

WHAT BUDDHISTS BELIEVE ABOUT GOD

Buddhism is often referred to as an atheistic religion. This description appears to be a contradiction of terms at first glance. However, it best describes the beliefs of Buddhists because they deny the existence of a Creator. According to Buddhists, there is no person, power, or being that is involved in controlling the universe. Buddhism teaches that nothing is eternal and absolute – not even God.

In Buddhism, the focus is on man, not on God. For the Buddhist, the existence of God is not important. Although statues of Buddha may be seen in gardens and at temples, Buddha taught his followers to look within themselves for the answers to life's problems.

Buddha taught his followers to look within themselves for the answers to life's problems.

WHAT BUDDHISTS BELIEVE ABOUT JESUS CHRIST

Amazingly, Buddhism began about 500 years before Jesus' birth. Although many Buddhists were around at the time of Jesus' birth, life, death, and resurrection, Jesus is basically ignored by Buddhists. And since they do not believe in God, Buddhists do not acknowledge that Jesus is God's son.

Most Buddhists will agree that Jesus was a good man because He lived a moral life. Also, many followers of Buddha will say that Jesus was a wise man. However, Jesus is never considered by them to be as wise or as moral as Buddha.

As Christians, we know that the Bible, in *John 1:1-3*, teaches that Jesus was much more than just a good man. These verses tell us that Jesus was also God, and that He was with God in the beginning.

Many people then began to follow the teachings of Buddha. Even today many people look to the writing of the Buddha for wisdom and the answers to life's problems.

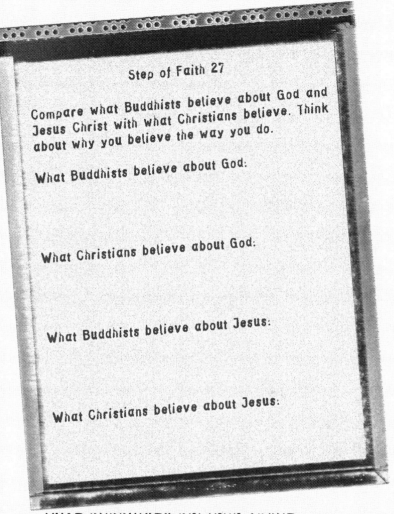

Step of Faith 27

Compare what Buddhists believe about God and Jesus Christ with what Christians believe. Think about why you believe the way you do.

What Buddhists believe about God:

What Christians believe about God:

What Buddhists believe about Jesus:

What Christians believe about Jesus:

WHAT BUDDHISTS BELIEVE ABOUT SALVATION AND LIFE AFTER DEATH

According to Buddhism, a person does not have a soul. People are reincarnated over and over again. The present life a person is living is the result of past lives. Buddhists believe that the act of living will always include pain, suffering, sickness, and disease. For Buddhists, these things must be endured in their present life and in future lifetimes. Since the root cause of this suffering is desire or ego, the goal of Buddhism is to eliminate desire and thus escape suffering. This is done by following the system called "the eightfold path." The eightfold path contains eight ways of right living which one must do in order to escape this world and reach nirvana. Nirvana is an escape from the cycle of suffering, birth, and death. Nirvana is not necessarily a place, but the end of suffering. Buddhism stresses that this escape from the world that they call nirvana is strictly within the power of the individual. The Buddhist relies on Buddha and his teaching for direction. His teachings give the only help for escaping the endless cycle of reincarnation. The Buddhist believes he has been trapped in this cycle for thousands of years. There are no prayers to say or a God to help the individual. The Buddhist's great hope is that someday he will escape life.

"My parents think they have lived thousands of lives. They think that each lifetime influences their next life," Carolyn explained. *"I know it sounds weird."*

"I've always heard about people believing in reincarnation. I've just never known anyone who believes it," Heather said with a puzzled look on her face.

"They also say they are trying to reach nirvana. This is kind of like their salvation; it's the end of suffering."

"So, they don't understand at all when you talk about heaven, do they?" Todd asked.

"No way! Nirvana isn't really a place like we think of heaven. They think they must follow the

---

Sidenote: Nirvana is an escape from the cycle of suffering, birth, and death. Nirvana is not necessarily a place, but the end of suffering.

teaching of Buddha to reach nirvana. They will never understand salvation through Jesus, or heaven either," Carolyn said. "See what I'm talking about now? It's so frustrating trying to explain Christianity to them."

"Don't say they will never understand. They've been Buddhists their whole lives. It's hard to make a change after such a long time of believing one way," Kristi answered.

"Yeah, remember that there is always hope," Heather smiled. "Nothing is impossible with God!"

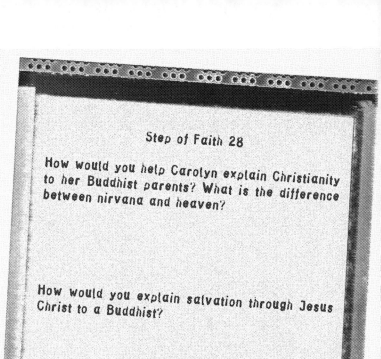

WHAT IS THEIR SCRIPTURE?

Buddhist scripture is usually divided into three types. The Vinaya gives the rules, regulations, and orders of the Buddhist faith. The Sutra contains sermons and general discussions between Buddha and his disciples. The Abhidharma includes philosophies and interpretations of others on the teachings of Buddha. Together, these three works make up the Tripitaka, or the Three Baskets, which is the Buddhist canon. The Tripitaka is about 11 times larger than our Bible!

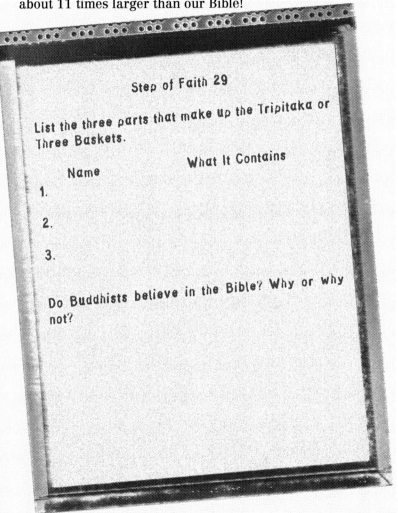

Step of Faith 29

List the three parts that make up the Tripitaka or Three Baskets.

　　　Name　　　　　　What It Contains

1.

2.

3.

Do Buddhists believe in the Bible? Why or why not?

FOUR NOBLE TRUTHS AND THE EIGHTFOLD PATH

The Four Noble Truths of Buddhism were developed by Buddha himself after he believed he had been enlightened. The Four Noble Truths of Buddhism are these: (1) suffering is universal; (2) the cause of suffering is selfish desire; (3) the cure for suffering is to eliminate selfish desire; and (4) the way to eliminate selfish desire is by following the eightfold path.

The Middle Way is the eightfold path which leads eventually to nirvana. The eight steps are: (1) right view, (2) right desires, (3) right speech, (4) right conduct, (5) right occupation, (6) right effort, (7) right awareness, and (8) right meditation.

The Middle Way is the eightfold path which leads eventually to nirvana.

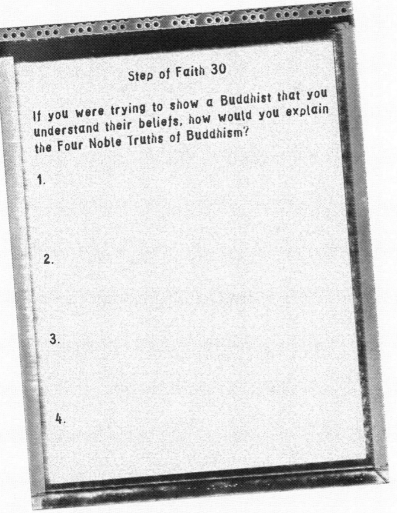

MORE OF BUDDHA'S TEACHINGS

Because Buddha preached a religion which had no authority figure, nowhere in Buddha's teachings does he mention worshiping God. According to Buddha, a person must find the answers within himself. There is no God or power to turn to for help. One must rely only upon himself.

Interestingly, Buddha preached a religion without rituals. Although he taught that the eightfold path would lead to nirvana, there is no set way of accomplishing the eight steps. Again, the results are totally up to the individual. There are no required prayers or chants to say. There is no chronological order of following the eightfold path. Each person must decide for himself the path or order which is right.

Also, Buddha preached a religion without speculation. He did not begin to guess or speculate on things. He did not allow his disciples to think about unanswerable questions. His disciples were not allowed to debate an issue and take opposing sides. He followed simple reasoning to answer the questions of life. Buddha believed that the things which could be useful in life and helpful in reaching nirvana were explainable. Anything else was wasted effort.

Just as Buddha preached a religion without ritual, he preached a religion void of traditions. He encouraged his followers to break free from the past. He taught them not to go by what is handed down or any traditional teachings. Instead, he encouraged his followers to find the answers for themselves and not to rely on the wisdom of others. One way he personally broke from tradition was by teaching in the language of the people and not the traditional Sanskrit language.

Buddha also preached a religion based on intense self-effort. He preached that no god or gods could be counted on, not even the Buddha himself. Every person must work at following the eightfold path based on his own energy and initiative. He believed that each person must find the power within himself to break the cycle of birth, death, and rebirth. The only way for a person to reach

Buddha also preached a religion based on intense self-effort.

nirvana was by following the eightfold path in his own way.

Finally, Buddha preached a religion void of the supernatural. His religion was based solely on reason and observable facts. He believed any problem or issue could be resolved by a person looking within himself for the answer. There was no need for a God to intervene or to perform miracles. Buddha told his followers to work out their own way to reach nirvana.

Step of Faith 31

Write down what Buddha taught about the following things.

1. Authority-

2. Rituals-

3. Speculation-

4. Traditions-

5. Self-effort-

6. Supernatural-

DO BUDDHISTS HAVE CHURCHES?

As Buddhism has come to the United States, it has Americanized itself by providing centers for meditation and retreat. It offers its followers temples, churches, and Sunday Schools. In the United States, Buddhism has become more missionary. It has adapted many ideas from American Christianity.

The Buddhist Churches of America hold their services on Sunday. They use the organ and piano in their worship services. One of the songs they sing in Sunday School is "Buddha loves me, this I know." A book called *The Teaching of Buddha* is distributed by this group.

The Japanese Buddhist religion called Nichiren Shoshu of America came to the United States in the 1960s. Nichiren Shoshu holds weekly meetings in homes or other buildings such as community centers. The services begin with chanting. This is followed by a unison reading of the Sutra, their scriptures. Then they sing songs pep-rally style. Testimonies are given by many of the Buddhist believers. People are invited to attend classes to help them learn how to chant the different words of the Sutra.

Zen Buddhism is probably the most influential form of Buddhism found in the United States. With Zen Buddhism, there is no God to worship, no rituals, no doctrine, no soul to worry about, and no need to worry about the souls of other people. Zen Buddhism is sometimes called the "religionless religion."

"Wow, Carolyn, you weren't kidding!" Todd said, shaking his head. "Buddhism is definitely different from Christianity."

Zen Buddhism is probably the most influential form of Buddhism found in the United States.

Step of Faith 32

Beside each of the following write BCA (Buddhist Churches of America), NSA (Nichiren Shoshu), or ZB (Zen Buddhism).

1. Uses organ and piano in worship ____
2. The "religionless" religion ____
3. Hold services on Sunday ____
4. Meets weekly in community center or home ____
5. Most influential form of Buddhism in the U.S. ____
6. Japanese form of Buddhism ____
7. Sings "Buddha loves me, this I know" ____
8. Give testimonies, sing, and chant ____

"Yeah, I had no idea it was so different," added Heather.

"Well, maybe now you guys can understand how hard it is for me at home. My parents believe so differently than I do," Carolyn said, "and they don't understand at all how I could believe in Jesus and accept Christian beliefs."

"It's going to be tough sharing your beliefs with them. Maybe we can help you come up with some way to break down the walls," Todd mentioned as he looked at Carolyn for approval.

"I know I can use all the help I can get."

Step of Faith 33

List some ways Carolyn could share Christ with her parents.

1.

2.

3.

How would you use the Bible to explain Christianity to a Buddhist?

What are some Bible verses you would share with a Buddhist?

GROUP LEARNING ACTIVITIES

These suggested Group Learning Activities are designed to secure active involvement of youth in the study of *Blind Faith: Living a Lie*. The activities have been developed with the assumption that, before each session, the youth will have read the assigned chapter and completed the Step of Faith activities. If this is not practical for your group, plan a time for youth to complete the activities during the session. Feel free to adapt the suggestions for the four one-hour sessions to the needs of your group.

For best results, youth leaders should carefully study the book and complete the Step of Faith activities in each chapter. Copies of the book should be ordered for all youth. Distribute the books prior to the first session.

SESSION 1

MORMONS: ARE THEY CHRISTIANS?

Session Goal: Youth will understand basic beliefs of Mormons and will be able to name specific reasons why they are not Christians.

AGENDA
1. **Are We Blind to the Truth? (10 Min.)**
2. **Making the Truth Clear (10)**
3. **Which Is the Truth? (15)**
4. **Defending the Truth (15)**
5. **Sharing the Truth (10)**

BEFORE THE SESSION
✔ ❑ Study the introduction and chapter 1 and complete the Step of Faith activities.
❑ Provide a bandanna or blindfold for every youth.
❑ Provide items for the opening activity. Suggested items include: various food items (especially fruit), whistle, stapler, bell, newspaper, book or magazine, sports equipment, types of cloth, etc. Place items in appropriate small group.
❑ Enlist four youth or youth leaders to facilitate the blindfold activity in small groups.
❑ Have a chalkboard and chalk or poster board and markers available.
❑ Have a large piece of paper on a focal wall. Place markers nearby.
❑ Have index cards and pencils available.

DURING THE SESSION
1. Are We Blind to the Truth?
As youth arrive, instruct them to get into four groups. All youth in the groups should put on blindfolds and begin to identify the items given to them by a group leader. One group will only smell various items. Another group will only be allowed to hear the sounds which the items make. A third group will be allowed to touch the items. The fourth group will only taste the items.
   Explain that although they could not see the items, they were able to identify many of them correctly. They had faith in what they could not

see. Explain that this is what these four sessions are all about. They will help youth to see Christianity in comparison with other world religions.

2. Making the Truth Clear
Direct youth to turn to Step of Faith 1 and complete it. Ask youth to share answers. Ask for youth to share if they have ever had to defend their faith to a Mormon.
Read *Mark 8:22-25*. Explain that just as the man did not see everything clearly at first, we may not either. Hopefully, as we study these sessions the truth will become clearer and we will be able to defend our faith more boldly.

3. Which Is the Truth?
Form three groups. Assign Step of Faith 2 to group 1. Assign Step of Faith 3 to group 2. Assign Step of Faith 4 and 5 to group 3. As they respond to their assigned activities, instruct them to review what they read in *Blind Faith* and to also use their Bibles. Reassemble into one large group and allow each group to share their answers.
Ask youth to brainstorm all they know about what Mormons believe. Write down their answers on one side of a chalkboard or poster board. Have youth do the same thing about what they believe as Christians. Write their answers on the opposite side of the chalkboard or poster board.
Ask youth to share how might someone be led to believe that Mormon beliefs are the truth.

4. Defending the Truth
Divide youth into two groups. Using the list you just compiled, have the groups debate. One group will represent Mormons and one group will defend Christianity. Youth may use their Bibles, *Blind*

Faith books, and Step of Faith activities.
Explain that defending our faith will not always be easy. It is really difficult to defend Christianity to someone who does not believe in the Bible. Ask youth to search their Bibles and find Scripture which supports one thing they believe as a Christian. Instruct youth to write the belief and the Scripture on a large piece of paper on a focal wall. Allow all youth to share why they believe Christianity is true.
Review the answers on the focal wall. Ask youth the following questions: (1) Why is Mormonism not a Christian denomination or religion? (2) How would you explain to a Mormon reasons he or she is not a Christian? (3) How would you explain to someone that the Mormon church is not the true church? Allow youth to give their answers as each question is asked.

5. <u>Sharing the Truth</u>
Direct youth to turn to Step of Faith 7. Ask youth to share their answers.
Ask youth to share other ways we can reach out to Mormons and share the truth with them.
Distribute index cards to youth. Ask youth to write down the name of one person who is a Mormon that they can be bolder in sharing their faith with this week. Have youth write down one way to reach out to that person before the next session. If youth do not know a Mormon, have them write down someone they know who is not a Christian.
Pray that each person will be firm in their faith and bolder about their Christianity, especially when faced with people of other religions.
Assign chapter 2 for the next session. Encourage youth to complete the Step of Faith activities.

SESSION 2

JEHOVAH'S WITNESSES: ARE THEY KNOCKING ON YOUR DOOR?

Session Goal: Youth will understand the basic beliefs of Jehovah's Witnesses and will be able to identify specific ways to witness to them.

AGENDA
1. Knocking On Your Door (10 Min.)
2. Who's Knocking? (10)
3. What Are They Teaching? (15)
4. Answering the Door (15)
5. Keeping the Door Open (10)

BEFORE THE SESSION
✔ ❑ Study chapter 2 and complete the Step of Faith activities.
❑ Have Bibles and *Blind Faith* books available.
❑ On a large banner print the title "Knocking On Your Door." Attach the banner to a focal wall. Place several colored markers nearby.
❑ Have index cards and pencils available.
❑ Have a chalkboard and chalk or poster board and markers available.

DURING THE SESSION
1. Knocking On Your Door
As youth arrive ask them to go to the "Knocking On Your Door" banner and write what they knew about Jehovah's Witnesses and their beliefs before reading this chapter. Youth may refer back to Step of Faith 8 in their *Blind Faith* book. After youth have written their answers, review the responses.

2. Who's Knocking?
Divide youth into two groups. Direct one group to

review Step of Faith 9. This group will role play the leadership of the Jehovah's Witnesses. Direct the other group to review Step of Faith 10. This group will role play the people who are attracted to Jehovah's Witnesses and their beliefs.

After both groups have rehearsed their role play, reassemble into one large group and have each group act out their role play.

Ask youth the following questions: (1) What do you think about a religion that is only a little over 100 years old? (2) How do you feel about the Watchtower Society? Do you think it is good for such a small group to have power and authority over so many people? (3) What do you think about the presidents serving for life? (4) Do you think Jehovah's Witnesses can really have the answers to life's problems? (5) Why do you think Jehovah's Witnesses are so committed to their beliefs?

3. <u>What Are They Teaching?</u>
Form three groups. Assign Step of Faith 11 to group 1. Assign Step of Faith 12 to group 2. Assign Step of Faith 13 to group 3. Instruct them to review what they read in *Blind Faith* and to use their Bibles. Reassemble into one large group and allow each group to share their answers.

Have youth compare what the Jehovah's Witnesses believe with Christianity. Compare beliefs about God, Jesus, salvation, and life after death. Discuss the differences that are found.

Ask youth to share reasons they believe people could be attracted to these beliefs of the Jehovah's Witnesses.

4. <u>Answering the Door</u>
Explain that defending Christianity to a Jehovah's Witness is a difficult thing. Remind youth that this

religious group is trained weekly at the Kingdom Hall to share their beliefs. However, as Christians, we must be ready to defend our faith when they come to our doors.

Ask youth to get into groups of four or five. Ask youth to search their Bibles and find Scripture which supports Christian beliefs that are opposite from what Jehovah's Witnesses believe. Youth may refer back to Step of Faith 14. Suggested topics or beliefs could include: the cross, the Holy Spirit, the name Jehovah, the physical resurrection of Jesus, or saluting the flag and showing allegiance to a nation. Have youth write down their answers and Scripture on index cards. They will be able to use the index cards during a debate.

Have each group share their answers with the large group.

Divide the youth into two groups. Again, look at the topics which the youth have just presented. Have the two groups debate the topics. One group will support the Christian viewpoint while the other group supports Jehovah's Witnesses.

Discuss ways the youth can defend their faith and still be able to share Christianity with a Jehovah's Witness.

5. Keeping the Door Open
Direct youth to turn to Step of Faith activities 15 and 16. Ask youth to share their answers.

On a large poster board or chalkboard, ask youth to brainstorm additional ways to reach out to Jehovah's Witnesses.

Explain that it will be difficult to share with Jehovah's Witnesses. They may not be involved in any school activities or community events because of what they believe. Youth will have to be very creative in reaching out to someone who is a

Jehovah's Witness. Ask youth to divide into groups of three. Instruct youth to pray for opportunities to build relationships with Jehovah's Witnesses. Also, have youth pray in their small groups for anyone they know who is a Jehovah's Witness. Have them pray that they will remain firm in their faith and be able to defend Christianity when they meet a Jehovah's Witness. Allow each group time to pray for additional prayer requests.

Assign chapter 3 for the next session. Encourage youth to complete the Step of Faith activities.

SESSION 3

MUSLIMS: WHY ARE THEY SO MYSTERIOUS?

Session Goal: Youth will understand basic beliefs of Muslims and discover ways to share Jesus Christ with them.

AGENDA
1. Mystery Words (10 Min.)
2. Solving the Mystery (15)
3. A Big Difference (15)
4. The Difference Is Jesus (10)
5. Ways to Share Christ (10)

BEFORE THE SESSION
✔
- ❏ Study chapter 3 and complete the Step of Faith activities.
- ❏ Prepare words for the "Mystery Words" activity and place in cups for each group.
- ❏ Enlist several youth to prepare a skit telling the story of *Genesis 16:1-16* and *Genesis 21:8-21*. Have the youth present the skit during the "A Big Difference" part of the session.
- ❏ Have a chalkboard and chalk or a large piece of

paper and markers available.
❑ Have another large piece of paper available. Divide the paper into two columns: "How Muslims and Christians Are Alike" and "How Muslims and Christians Are Different." Have markers available.

DURING THE SESSION

1. Mystery Words

As youth arrive, direct them to get into groups of five or six. Have one youth draw a word from a cup. The other youth may only ask questions that can be answered "yes" or "no." The youth will try to guess what the word is. The youth who guesses correctly gets to draw the next word and answer "yes" or "no" questions. (*Suggested words: camel, veil, Arab, prayer, or any other word which relates to the session.*)

After the youth have answered several words, bring everyone back to the large group. Explain that just as the words were mysteries and we had to guess what they were, many times Christians guess at what they think Muslims believe. Today's session will help you understand Muslims. By learning what Muslims believe, you can also learn how to better share Christ with them.

2. Solving the Mystery

Divide youth into three groups. Ask each group to develop a TV commercial which informs viewers about one Muslim belief. Have one group review "Who Are the Muslims and Muhammad?" and Step of Faith 18. Another group is to review "Who Is Their God?," "What About Jesus?," and Step of Faith 19. The other group will review "What Happens After Death?" and Step of Faith 20.

Have each group present their TV commercial.

Discuss the beliefs which were presented and compare them with Christianity. Discuss ways to explain Christian beliefs to a Muslim.

3. A Big Difference
Have the enlisted youth present their skit.
Explain that Muslims believe it was at this point that the Bible is wrong. They believe Ishmael went to the city of Mecca. Ask: Why do you think Muslims believe only part of the Bible? Have youth turn to Step of Faith 21. Discuss their answers.
Ask youth to think of ways to witness to a Muslim since they do not believe the Bible is totally accurate. List their answers on the chalkboard.

4. The Difference Is Jesus
Divide youth into three groups. Instruct the groups to review "The Practicing Muslim" and Step of Faith 22, and "Do Muslims Have Churches?" and Step of Faith 23. Have each group compare likenesses and differences of Muslims and Christians.
Have each group present their answers to the large group. As each group shares, have one youth write their answers on the large piece of paper labeled "How Muslims and Christians Are Alike" on one side and "How Muslims and Christians Are Different" on the other side.
Explain that even though there may be some similarities between Muslims and Christians (they both pray, give money, etc.) the differences are great. Explain that what each group believes about Jesus is the biggest difference. Discuss the differences between Muslims and Christians concerning their beliefs in Jesus.

5. Ways to Share Christ
Have youth review "Can You Share Christ With a

Muslim?" and Step of Faith 24. Ask youth to share their answers with the large group.

Discuss the following questions: (1) Does it do any good to share verses from the Bible with a Muslim? Why or why not? (2) How can you explain to a Muslim the difference that Christ makes in your life and the lives of other Christians? (3) How would you explain your church to a Muslim? Would you invite them to your church? Why or why not? (4) Do you know anyone who is Muslim? What can you do this week to share Christ with a Muslim or a person of another religion who does not believe in Jesus as their Savior?

After the group has discussed the questions, review the specific ways to share Christ with a Muslim. Encourage youth to be bold in their witness. Close in prayer with the large group. Pray for the millions of people in the world who do not know Christ, especially the large numbers of Muslims.

Assign chapter 4 for the next session. Encourage youth to complete the Step of Faith activities.

SESSION 4

BUDDHISTS: A RELIGION WITH NO GOD

Session Goal: Youth will understand the basic beliefs of Buddhists and will identify specific ways in which Buddhism differs from Christianity.

AGENDA
1. Who Is Buddha? (10 Min.)
2. No God? (10)
3. Three Baskets or the Bible? (15)
4. True or False? (15)
5. How Can You Share Jesus With a Buddhist? (10)

BEFORE THE SESSION

✔ ❏ Study chapter 4 and complete the Step of Faith activities.
❏ Have Bibles and *Blind Faith* books available.
❏ On a large banner, print the title "What Buddhists Believe." Attach the banner to a focal wall. Place several colored markers nearby.
❏ Enlist at least five youth to role play "Where Did Buddha Come From?" in *Blind Faith*. Youth will present the role play at the beginning of the session.
❏ Have a large piece of paper or newsprint available.
❏ Secure copies of four supermarket tabloid newspapers and four reliable newspapers.
❏ Have paper, markers, glue, scissors, and other supplies available to be used for making props or signs for television commercials.
❏ On a large banner, print the title "Buddhist Churches." Have the three types of Buddhism listed which are common to the United States. (Buddhist Churches of America, Nichiren Shoshu of America, and Zen Buddhism.)

DURING THE SESSION

1. Who Is Buddha?

As youth arrive, ask them to go to the "What Buddhists Believe" banner and write down what they knew about Buddhists and their beliefs before reading this chapter. Youth may refer back to Step of Faith 25. After all youth have written down their answers, review what they knew before the session.

Have previously enlisted youth role play "Where Did Buddha Come From?" from *Blind Faith*. Discuss how Buddhism began and review Step of Faith 26.

2. No God?
Divide youth into two groups. Have one group review "What Buddhists Believe About God" and Step of Faith 27. The second group will review "What Buddhists Believe About Jesus Christ" and Step of Faith 27. Allow each group to present their answers. Have one youth write answers on a large piece of paper or newsprint.
As a whole group, review "What Buddhists Believe About Salvation And Life After Death." Discuss Step of Faith 28 answers.

3. Three Baskets or the Bible?
Divide youth into four groups. Give each group one tabloid newspaper and one reliable newspaper. Ask youth to review major stories in each paper. Then have one youth from each group report on one or two of the stories in each paper.
Ask: "If it is in print, does that make it truth?" Allow youth to discuss their answers.
Have youth review "What Is Their Bible?" and Step of Faith 29. Discuss what characteristics are necessary to make a book of faith reliable.

4. True or False?
Divide youth into six groups. Have the groups review "Four Noble Truths and The Eight-fold Path," "More of Buddha's Teachings," and Step of Faith 30 and 31.
Instruct each group to come up with a one-minute television commercial which advertises Buddha's teachings from Step of Faith 31. Make sure each group has a different teaching to advertise. Have extra paper, markers, scissors, glue, and other supplies available to be used for props. Allow the groups to present their commercials.
Review the teachings of Buddha in comparison

with Christian teachings. Discuss the major differences in the two religions.

5. How Can You Share Jesus With a Buddhist?
Direct youth to the "Buddhist Churches" banner on the wall. Have youth call out common characteristics of the three types of Buddhism found in America. As youth give their answers, have one youth write the answers on the banner. Youth may refer back to "Do Buddhists Have Churches?" and Step of Faith 32 in *Blind Faith*.

As a large group answer the questions in Step of Faith 33. Discuss ways to share Jesus Christ with a Buddhist. Use the following questions for discussion: (1) How can you use the Bible to explain Christianity if the Buddhist does not believe the Bible? (2) What is the purpose of using verses from the Bible if the Buddhist does not believe the Bible? (3) How would you explain God to a Buddhist? (4) How would you defend your Christianity to a Buddhist?

Answer Key for Step of Faith Activities

CHAPTER 1: SOF 1-Your answers. SOF 2-Your answers. SOF 3-Your answers. SOF 4-Your answers. SOF 5-M;M;C;M;C;M;C;M. SOF 6-Jesus; Body of believers in Christ; Your answers. SOF 7-Your answers.

CHAPTER 2: SOF 8-Your answers. SOF 9-C;A;D;B. SOF 10-Your answers. SOF 11-Your answers. SOF 12-Your answers. SOF 13-Good works; Two; The Anointed; Special spiritual privileges; Born; Other sheep; Earth; Death. SOF 14-Your answers. SOF 15-Your answers. SOF 16-Your answers.

CHAPTER 3: SOF 17-Your answers. SOF 18-True; True; False; True; False; False. SOF 19-Your answers. SOF 20-Your answers. SOF 21-Your answers. SOF 22-Profession of faith; Pray five times a day; Give 2 1/2 percent of income to government; Fast during the month of Ramadan; Go to Mecca at least once during their lifetime; Be willing to fight in war for Allah. SOF 23-Your answers. SOF 24-Your answers.

CHAPTER 4: SOF 25-Your answers. SOF 26-True; False; True; True; False; True; False. SOF 27-Your answers. SOF 28-Your answers. SOF 29-Vinaya; Rules, regulations, orders; Sutra; Sermons and discussions with disciples of Buddha; Abhidharma; Philosophies and interpretations of Buddha's teachings; No; They do not believe in God, Jesus, or the Bible. SOF 30-Your answers. SOF 31-Your answers. SOF 32-BCA;ZB;BCA;NSA; ZB;NSA;BCA; NSA. SOF 33-Your answers.

CONCLUSION

Hopefully, as you have read the preceding pages you have developed an informed Christian faith. As you study the factuality of Scripture, the historical facts regarding the birth, life, death, and resurrection of Jesus Christ, and the reasons Christians believe what they do, you will have a greater understanding and appreciation for the statement in Hebrews:

> *Now faith is being sure of what we hope for and certain of what we do not see.*
> *Hebrews 11:1*

To be sure of what we hope for and certain of what we do not see is informed faith. To accept something just because someone said it is so is blind faith. May your faith always have sight and be blessed by Him Who is Light.

And now,

> *To him who is able to keep you from falling and to present you before his glorious presence without fault and with great joy – to the only God our Savior be glory, majesty, power and authority, through Jesus Christ our Lord, before all ages, now and forevermore! Amen.*
> *Jude 24-25*

ADDITIONAL RESOURCES

To obtain Interfaith Witness resources contact: North American Mission Board of the Southern Baptist Convention, 4200 North Point Parkway, Alpharetta, GA 30022-4176, or you may visit them at www/namb.net/evangelism/IEV

We've got answers!

Students are looking for purpose and meaning in life. Too many are turning to secular, humanistic worldviews to find the answers to some basic life questions.

Clearly, Scripture provides solid answers to each of these questions; and through this new study, Chuck Colson guides students to understand what the Bible has to say regarding these real-life questions. *How Now Shall We Live?* provides a biblical foundation for students to build their lives upon; and they'll never look at life the same way again once they've experienced this kind of truth!

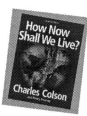

How Now Shall We Live? Student Edition   (0-6330-0451-0) $10.95
Designed to help the cynical-yet-searching youth understand and deal with the secular worldviews that permeate every aspect of today's society. Challenging, lively, and fun — with an edge, of course. Contains materials for eight sessions.

How Now Shall We Live? Leader's Guide   (0-6330-0450-2) $6.95
Includes administrative helps and learning activities. Enhances what students learn on their own.

How Now Shall We Live? Video   (0-6330-0390-5) $39.95
Allows your students to see and hear from Colson and students like themselves who have found biblical answers to many of life's toughest issues. Fun and informative, this video is designed to be used with the Leader's Guide and Student Edition.

5 WAYS TO ORDER:
Toll-free: **1-800-458-2772**   Automated: **1-800-376-1140**
Internet: **www.lifeway.com**   Email: **customerservice@lifeway.com**
or visit the LifeWay Christian Store serving you!

OMO # A461A99